My English Port f...

Name: ....

Surname: ....

Age: ....

Address: ....

....

School: ....

Class: ....

Teacher: ....

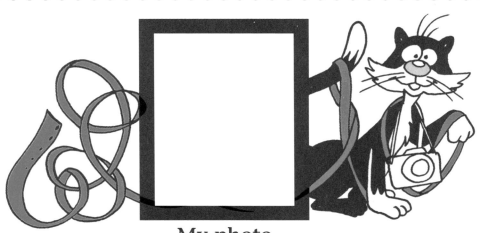

My photo

1 Welcome back!

I can ...

		Good	Very good	Excellent
Recognise and say the names of 10 colours	What I think	☐	☐	☐
	What my teacher thinks	☐	☐	☐
Write the names of 10 colours	What I think	☐	☐	☐
	What my teacher thinks	☐	☐	☐
Recognise and say the names of animals	What I think	☐	☐	☐
	What my teacher thinks	☐	☐	☐
Write the names of animals	What I think	☐	☐	☐
	What my teacher thinks	☐	☐	☐

1 **Read and colour.**

a brown ruler • yellow scissors • a red rubber

2 **Read and draw.**

A pink rabbit is jumping.

A blue dog is shaking his legs.

A yellow cat is eating ice cream

...it's OK, it's just a dream!

2 All year round

I can ...

		Good	Very good	Excellent
Recognise and say the days of the week	What I think	☐	☐	☐
	What my teacher thinks	☐	☐	☐
Recognise and say the seasons and months of the year	What I think	☐	☐	☐
	What my teacher thinks	☐	☐	☐
Use expressions to talk about the weather	What I think	☐	☐	☐
	What my teacher thinks	☐	☐	☐
Ask when someone's birthday is	What I think	☐	☐	☐
	What my teacher thinks	☐	☐	☐

1 Write the days of the week.

S D A Y U N ....

T H R D S U A Y ....

F D I R A Y ....

M O D N Y A ....

W D E S N E A Y D ....

S T A R D U A Y ....

T E U D S Y A ....

2 Answer the questions.

What do you do on Monday? ....

What do you do on Saturday afternoon? ....

What do you do when it's raining? ....

What do you do when it's sunny? ....

What's your favourite day? ....

3 Going shopping

I can ...

		Good	Very good	Excellent
Recognise and say the numbers to 100	What I think	☐	☐	☐
	What my teacher thinks	☐	☐	☐
Write the numbers to 100	What I think	☐	☐	☐
	What my teacher thinks	☐	☐	☐
Ask how much an object costs and respond	What I think	☐	☐	☐
	What my teacher thinks	☐	☐	☐

1 **Write the numbers.**

eighteen
☐

ninety-two
☐

seventy-four
☐

fifteen
☐

sixty-three
☐

eleven
☐

ninety-four
☐

thirty-five
☐

seventy-one
☐

eighty-six
☐

thirty
☐

sixty-six
☐

2 **Answer the questions.**

How many weeks are there in a year? ....

How many books have you got in your bedroom? ....

How many pupils are there in your class? ....

How many chairs are there in your classroom? ....

My shopping list

3 Imagine you are shopping in London.
Write a list of things you want to buy. Draw pictures.

4 Now write a dialogue. You want to buy something but you have only got fifteen pounds.

You	The shop assistant
....	....
....	....
....	....
....	....
....	....

4 Dreams

I can ...

		Good	Very good	Excellent
Talk and write about my dreams	What I think	☐	☐	☐
	What my teacher thinks	☐	☐	☐
Use adverbs of frequency: never, sometimes, often, always	What I think	☐	☐	☐
	What my teacher thinks	☐	☐	☐
Use prepositions: in, on, under, behind	What I think	☐	☐	☐
	What my teacher thinks	☐	☐	☐

1 **Write the words.**

...........flying...........   ....

....

2 **Write about your dreams.**

I often dream about ....

I never dream about ....

I sometimes dream about ....

I always dream about ....

8

3 Draw your bedroom. Then write.

| in | on | under | behind |

....

....

....

....

I can ...

Good

Very good

Excellent

		Good	Very good	Excellent
Ask and say what time it is	What I think	☐	☐	☐
	What my teacher thinks	☐	☐	☐
Talk about routines	What I think	☐	☐	☐
	What my teacher thinks	☐	☐	☐

1 **Read and complete the clocks.**

It's seven
o'clock.

It's quarter
past six.

It's half
past two.

It's five
o'clock.

It's quarter
to ten.

It's half
past eight.

It's quarter
past nine.

It's ten
o'clock.

My day

2 Draw your favourite time of day.

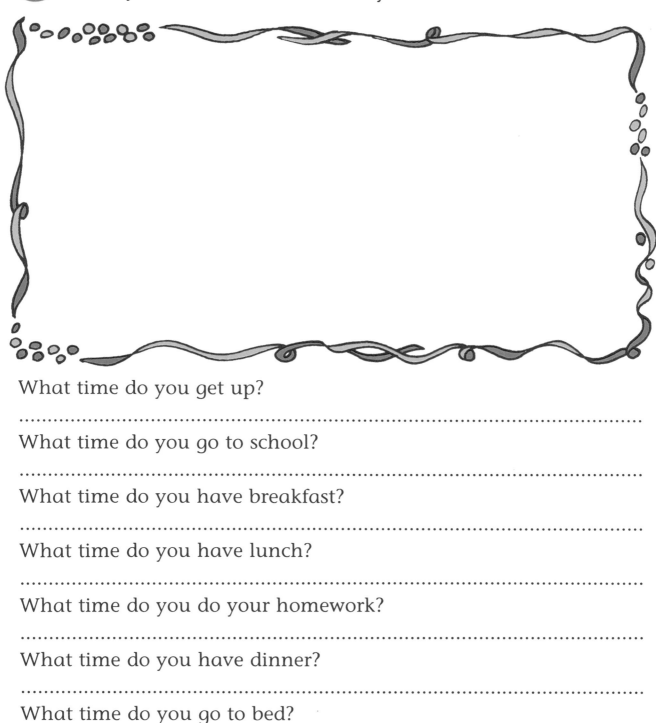

What time do you get up?

....

What time do you go to school?

....

What time do you have breakfast?

....

What time do you have lunch?

....

What time do you do your homework?

....

What time do you have dinner?

....

What time do you go to bed?

....

6 Television

I can ...

Good

Very good

Excellent

		Good	Very good	Excellent
Recognise and say the names of different types of television programmes	What I think	☐	☐	☐
	What my teacher thinks	☐	☐	☐
Write the names of different types of television programmes	What I think	☐	☐	☐
	What my teacher thinks	☐	☐	☐
Say what time a programme starts	What I think	☐	☐	☐
	What my teacher thinks	☐	☐	☐

1 Circle the programmes.
The other words make a question. Write your answer.

WHATCARTOONSISQUIZSHOWSYOURTHENEWSFAVOURITEROMANTICFILMSPROGRAMME?

....

2 Look and write.

She likes .... She doesn't like ....

He likes .... He doesn't like ....

My favourite programmes

3 Draw your favourite television programme.
Answer the questions.

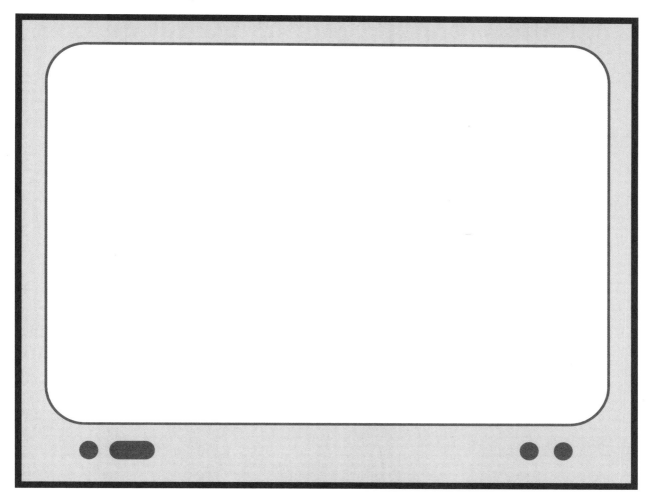

What do you watch on Monday? ....

What do you watch on Sunday? ....

What's your favourite programme? ....

What time does your favourite programme start? ....

What programme do you never watch? ....

What programme do you always watch? ....

I can ...

		Good	Very good	Excellent
Recognise and say the names of different leisure activities	What I think	☐	☐	☐
	What my teacher thinks	☐	☐	☐
Write the names of different leisure activities	What I think	☐	☐	☐
	What my teacher thinks	☐	☐	☐

1 Tick *true* or *false*.

Tom is swimming.

True   False
☐   ☐

They are lying
in the sun.

True   False
☐   ☐

Timmy is reading.

True   False
☐   ☐

Janet is riding
a horse.

True   False
☐   ☐

They are listening
to music.

True   False
☐   ☐

They are playing.

True   False
☐   ☐